BRIAN JOHNSTON

Incredible Unbelief

... when believing nothing means believing anything ...

First published by Hayes Press 2022

Copyright © 2022 by Brian Johnston

All rights reserved. No part of this publication may be reproduced, stored or transmitted in any form or by any means, electronic, mechanical, photocopying, recording, scanning, or otherwise without written permission from the publisher. It is illegal to copy this book, post it to a website, or distribute it by any other means without permission.

Brian Johnston asserts the moral right to be identified as the author of this work.

Unless otherwise stated, all Bible quotations are taken from the (NASB®) New American Standard Bible®, Copyright © 1960, 1971, 1977, 1995, 2020 by The Lockman Foundation. Used by permission. All rights reserved. www.lockman.org

First edition

This book was professionally typeset on Reedsy. Find out more at reedsy.com

Between 1900 and 2000 over 65% of Nobel Prize-winners were self-confessed believers in God. One of them reacted with the following statement when asked about his view of origins:

"The best data we have are exactly what I would have predicted, had I nothing to go on but the five Books of Moses, the Psalms, the Bible as a whole."

Arno Penzias, Nobel Prize winner and co-discoverer of background radiation

Preface

Atheistic scientists like Richard Dawkins admit that science has no "strongly satisfying" explanation for why the universe appears to have been fine-tuned with the precise conditions ideally suited to life as we know it, but he urges his readers (*The God Delusion*, pp.157,158) "not to give up hope" in "some kind of multiverse theory." This refers to the totally speculative idea that a trillion trillion parallel universes exist simply to explain the remote chance of this one being exactly as it is. In this unpublicized section of his best-selling book, Dawkins appeals to his readers not to give up hope in the discovery of some new scientific theory that will one day save atheism!

On the other hand, the best-selling book that is the Bible says: "*that which is known about God is evident ... for God made it evident ... for since the creation of the world His invisible attributes ... have been clearly seen ... through what has been made ... [but] they did not honour Him as God ... but they became futile in their speculations*" (Romans 1:19-21).

I

The Failure of any 'God-less Hypothesis'

It cannot explain:
1 Something Out of Nothing (The Origin of the Universe)
2 The Origin of Stars
3 The Origin of Life
4 The Origin of Biodiversity
5 The Origin of Mind and Morality

1

Something Out of Nothing

Something out of nothing – is that how the universe began? The front cover of *Discover* magazine (April 2002) once announced that: "The universe burst into something from absolutely nothing—zero, nada. And as it got bigger, it became filled with even more stuff that came from absolutely nowhere." In this way, the so-called Big Bang story tries to explain the beginning of the universe. It's obvious that the universe couldn't have come from the same sort of stuff as our present universe, because then that matter or energy would also have needed to have a beginning, only one that was further back in time.

That leaves the option that it had to come from nothing! In other words, nothing became everything with no known cause whatsoever. You'd be correct in thinking that's a magical belief. For those who would acknowledge nothing beyond the existence of material things, there's no explanation for the origin of the universe. Effectively, what they say is "it must have happened because we're here!" In other words, it happened just like magic: just like the proverbial rabbit out of the hat. Only, in the case of the universe, that's a rather large "rabbit"!

There are other aspects of the Big Bang, the accepted story of our universe's origin, that are equally miraculous. What's known as the "standard model" has a period of very rapid expansion referred to as "inflation." This involves more magic, because there's no known cause for how this supposed expansion began since it requires an enormous input of energy. There's also no known physical mechanism for how it could produce an expansion of space itself that's faster than the speed of light. However, these related miracles *must have happened* or else the Big Bang idea simply doesn't work.[1]

Operational science, on the other hand, tests events that are repeatable, and history isn't repeatable. The Big Bang story requires immense imagination (as well as conveniently overlooking galaxies that are observed to cluster together and appear to be billions of years more mature than the Big Bang story predicts). How the universe got started is just one of five major examples of atheists believing in miracles without having any explanation for them – and we'll be looking at all five of them in the opening chapters of this book.

But, in case you think I'm presenting some kind of maverick view, here's what was said when the *New Scientist* published a letter signed by 33 top scientists that had the title "Bucking the Big Bang": "Big bang theory relies on a growing number of ... things that we have never observed. Inflation, dark matter and dark energy are the most prominent. Without them, there would be fatal contradictions between the observations made by astronomers and the predictions of the big bang theory. In no other field of physics would this continual resource to new hypothetical objects be accepted as a way of bridging the gap between theory and observation."

It really is like the little boy who said: "Let me get this straight. First there was nothing ... and then it exploded?" That's a fair cop. You can't get something from nothing. And that means we have to ask how could anything exist unless Someone put it there? This question has been used as a classic argument for the existence of God—an argument that theoretical physicist Lawrence Krauss tried to tackle in his book *A Universe from Nothing*.

He explains the "nothing" that the universe came from as being a sea of energy obeying some very special laws of (quantum) physics (a "quantum vacuum"). But nothing is supposed to mean just that—"no thing," in other words, the complete absence of any matter or energy or force or space or laws of physics. I'm afraid a sea of energy obeying some very special laws of physics is not "nothing." Matter and energy are interchangeable, and so it's a very definite something, and we'd have to ask: "How did *it* come to be there?"

We mentioned a Someone a moment ago, and that brings us to the alternative idea about how the universe began. For that Someone is described in the Bible:

> *"HOLY, HOLY, HOLY is THE LORD GOD, THE ALMIGHTY, WHO WAS AND WHO IS AND WHO IS TO COME"* (Revelation 4:8).

> *"Worthy are You, our Lord and our God, to receive glory and honor and power; for You created all things, and because of Your will they existed, and were created"* (Revelation 4:11).

In two places in the Old Testament (Isaiah 12:1; 26:4), the text essentially repeats God's name as Yah Yahweh (or Jah Jehovah). The Hebrew language uses the duplication of words for emphasis. God's unchanging character is being stressed. God is. He just is. There's no other like God. We, his creatures, are different. We're creatures completely defined by change. We're not really human beings; we're human becomings. Greek thinkers had it right when they said "Whatever is, is" and "What is not, cannot become" (Parmenides). In other words, you need a supreme being before a universe – or anything else – can ever become, that is, come into existence. Or to borrow from historic Christian teachers, God is not only the supreme Being, but he is a necessary Being. What that's saying is: God absolutely must be; he simply cannot NOT be! For if God were to cease to be, the universe would vaporize and just disappear.

Looking at it the other way round, this has been used as a classic argument for the existence of God. For, suppose God did not exist, and that there once truly was "not anything" (not even a sea of energy obeying scientific laws) – then there still would be and could only be nothing now. There is no such thing as a "free lunch." You can't get something out of nothing. Not spontaneously; and not in 13.7 billion years. To believe otherwise, as we've seen, is to believe in magic – in fact it's worse than that. It would be like pulling a rabbit out of a hat – without the hat, and without the magician!

It's God's unique prerogative to bring something out of nothing. Revelation 4:11, already mentioned, says God created all things and because of his sovereign will they came into existence, into being. There's no other possible, logical or scientific explanation. More recently, some (e.g. Stephen Hawking) have put forward the idea that the universe created itself. However, there's a pretty basic problem with the idea of a universe that creates itself. For, in order to do so, it must violate the Law of Non-Contradiction. What do I mean by that? Well, the Law of Non-Contradiction has got to be one of the most intuitive and self-evidently obvious of all laws. It simply says: "something cannot be both green and not green at the same time."

You can, of course, substitute anything in place of the colour green I used in that example. For instance, a universe cannot both exist and not exist at the same time. But that's exactly what's implied by a universe that somehow creates itself. It needs to exist in order to do the creating; but it also must not exist so as to be brought into existence. To both exist and not exist at the same time breaks the Law of Non-Contradiction. It's nonsense. And to escape such nonsense, we need only turn to the famous opening lines of the Bible: *"In the beginning God created the heavens and the earth"* (Genesis 1:1). This isn't magic, because God, who is eternal and omnipotent, is a *sufficient cause* for the universe. And he can exist eternally (and therefore has no beginning) because he is a non-material entity (God is spirit, as the Bible says in many places). By the way, the opening ten words of the Bible collide head-on with the major assumption that lies behind the Big Bang story – and that assumption is the one that says the earth isn't a special place.

Why do apparently intelligent people resort to believing in magic—uncaused events—at so many points? The Apostle Paul says in the Bible (in Romans 1:21) that when people deny that the Creator-God exists, they end up with "futile thinking." Nothing makes more sense than: *"In the beginning God created the heavens and the earth."* This is because the idea of an original "singularity" cannot be explained in terms of the current laws of physics. It's where they break down. So it's a problem for science.

Footnote:

1. Background microwave radiation is all around us - beaming down on us from space all around (this was famously discovered in 1964/5 by Penzias & Wilson). We've also discovered that it's at the same temperature everywhere. To get to such a stable state of things after an explosive start would take much longer than the usual estimated age of the universe because energy would need to have travelled from warmer areas to cooler ones (and that, too, is something that's limited by the speed of light) so as to make them all the same temperature as we observe today. And that's where the miracle of inflation comes in. It solves this by imagining that different regions of the universe were in very close contact before the inflation took place – meaning that then they were able to come to the same temperature by exchanging radiation before they were rapidly pushed apart.

2

The Origin of Stars

It's wonderful to see the stars on a dark night when we're far away from the streetlights of any city. Some of the best views I've had of the heavens have been from the African continent. Many years ago I invested in a small telescope but it soon became clear that using it from my home was pretty much useless – other than for viewing the moon close up. For other viewings, there's too much local "light pollution," not to mention the mist and fog that so often gathers in the low-lying land where we live. If you've seen photographs of the stars of our Milky Way galaxy – photographs that have been shot at night from the bottom of a canyon, in the United States, for example, you'll surely agree that they're an awesome sight.

But have you ever thought of how they were formed? The first chapter of the Bible uses an impressive economy of words to describe the creation of the stars by God. It simply says: He made the "*stars too.*" Two words only in the original language! That's the height of understatement, is it not? The universe around us is vast. Perhaps it's worth me trying to give you some sense of the grand scale of the universe. There's a way of doing this that's quite neat. If we're going to measure some large object, we need – or we used to need – an item for comparison that had a very well-known standard length. For example, in school we used to use the schoolboys' standard twelve-inch ruler or a yardstick, marked out as exactly three feet in the old system of imperial units that used to be commonplace in the United Kingdom. Well, to measure the universe, we're going to need some kind of gigantic "ruler," a massive "yardstick." In other words, we need a standard unit of length that's big enough for the job in hand, namely measuring the entire universe.

What's the longest distance that we can easily imagine? That would probably be the distance from where we stand on earth all the way to the sun we daily see overhead in the sky. What if we make that our standard unit of length and use it as a measuring tool? Let's call it "one astronomical unit" and see how we go on. Astronomers are confident they know the distance from the earth to the sun, and tell us it's 93 million miles. So, that's one unit. Now, here's where it gets neat, owing to a strange coincidence. There are the same number of inches in a mile (that would be 63,000) as there are astronomical units in the total distance travelled by light in one year – which we call a light-year.

Let's work everything on that scale where one inch represents one astronomical unit (AU). We start with the earth, and so the sun is 1 inch away. Our nearest star would then be more than four (4.4) miles away (it's called Alpha Centauri). And our nearest (big) galaxy is over two (2.3) million miles away (known as the Andromeda galaxy). And, of course, these are only the nearest objects! We might well ask: "Why is the universe as big as it is?" That question is particularly relevant if we as Christians believe God's purpose in creation was primarily to create a habitable environment for his human creation. Psalm 14 begins by saying: "*The heavens declare the glory of God.*" That probably gives us some clue as to why the universe is so big. Nothing smaller could adequately convey anything of the glory of God.

Well then, the universe is gigantic, beyond the ability of most of us to imagine. Modern science does try to estimate or make a good guess at the number of galaxies the universe contains. Our own backyard galaxy is the Milky Way, but it's thought there could be one hundred thousand million other such galaxies. That's a 1 with 11 zeros after it. What's more, we might suppose there's the same number of stars in each and every galaxy – at least on average. Put those two factoids together and you would get a possible total guess of the number of stars in the universe as being a 1 followed by 22 zeros. Remember, we think of a million as being a big number, but that's a 1 followed by only 6 zeros. Here we're talking about a 1 followed by 22 zeros – the possible number of stars in the universe - but remember it's only a guess.

But how did the stars form in the first place? Well that's a bit of a mystery, a major mystery in fact. We often hear of how the universe is expanding. There's evidence that can be interpreted in that way. But here's the thing. We learn in school about how the early universe contained only the lightest gases, hydrogen and helium. But gas clouds in an expanding universe won't collapse to form stars. That's because gases don't tend to come together. Instead of coming together, they disperse, especially where there's a lot of heat energy about. To bring about any collapse, the Big Bang story – a term that I'm sure is familiar to most, if not all, of us – invents the miracle of something called "dark matter." It's "dark" because we haven't been able to directly detect its existence. This invisible and undetected "stuff" is something that needs to be imagined in order to generate a lot of gravitational attraction to compensate for the expansion of hot gas clouds. It's all so that these dusty clouds condense under the action of gravity, which as we know is the force that draws things together.

Bible-believing Christians have been scorned for believing in a "God of the gaps" - the criticism being that the only reason we needed God was to fill in the gaps science couldn't explain. For some, it seemed that as science became more sophisticated those gaps were shrinking and soon God wouldn't be needed at all as a fall-back explanation. In reality, the gaps have simply been filled with things like "dark matter." That also takes faith. Atheistic answers are "stuff happens" and "it's Nature's way" – that's science of the gaps: it's belief in things for which we've no evidence.

In the first part of this book, we're exploring five major examples of atheists (materialists) believing in magic – if we use that term to describe miraculous events happening without any sufficient explanation or cause for those events. *"In the beginning God created the heavens and the earth"* (Genesis 1:1). This is not magic, because God, who is eternal and omnipotent, is a *sufficient cause* for the universe. And he can exist eternally (and therefore has no beginning) because he is a non-material being (God is spirit, as the Bible says).

According to the Big Bang, and it's the "only game in town" in the world of secular science, in order to explain the origin of stars there had to have been two phases or stages of star formation. The first involved the formation of hydrogen or helium stars (and we've already mentioned the difficulty with that). But, moving on, we also have countless stars—like our sun—that are not just hydrogen and helium, but they contain the heavier elements. That's where the second phase supposedly comes in. Exploding stars (known as supernovas) are said to have once produced sufficient pressure to force hydrogen and helium together to make new stars that then made all the heavier elements (which astronomers call "metals"), including the elements we are made of.

Which brings us to another problem: how do exploding stars, with stuff flying in all directions at great speed, cause stars to be made from all those new elements? There has to be a coming together of the elements, not a flying apart. Pieces hitting one another would bounce off rather than stick. Most ideas involve lots of supernovas in close proximity to make sure enough stuff collided together to form a proto-star with sufficient gravity to overcome the tendency to fly apart. However, supernovas are not common events, never mind lots of them happening close together at the same time! In short, we can see how this idea requires a large number of very unlikely events to explain the vast numbers of heavier stars.

This is more magic: miracles without a miracle worker. The famous (and reluctant) convert from Atheism to Christianity, C.S. Lewis, put it well when he wrote, "If the solar system was brought about by an accidental collision, then the appearance of organic life on this planet was also an accident, and the whole evolution of Man was an accident too. If so, then all our present thoughts are mere accidents—the accidental by-product of the movement of atoms. And this holds for the thoughts of the materialists and astronomers as well as for anyone else's. But if *their* thoughts—i.e. of materialism and astronomy—are merely accidental by-products, why should we believe them to be true? I see no reason for believing that one accident should be able to give me a correct account of all the other accidents. It's like expecting that the accidental shape taken by the splash when you upset a milk jug should give you a correct account of how the jug was made and why it was upset." So said C. S. Lewis. Good point.

The Bible book of Genesis says that God made the sun and the stars on the fourth day of Creation Week. This is neither magic nor superstition, because God is able to do such things: "*It is He who ... stretches out the heavens like a curtain and spreads them out like a tent to live in ... Raise your eyes on high and see who has created these stars, the One who brings out their multitude by number, He calls them all by name; because of the greatness of His might and the strength of His power, not one of them is missing*" (Isaiah 40:22-26). But, for sure, you must first believe the God of the Bible exists – and is the rewarder of all who seek him (Hebrews 11:6).

3

The Origin of Life

Some strident atheist voices today are quite mistaken as to the true nature of faith, and seem to think it's only some kind of poor substitute for evidence. They keep demanding that we should go by empirical results – meaning opinions based on experience and observation rather than vague theory. Well then, science at its most empirical says life comes from life - life doesn't come from non-life.

The ancient Greeks had once believed that small animals such as worms, mice, and maggots sprang to life automatically from the non-living matter around (such as rotting flour, a sweaty shirt, or decaying meat). This belief that living matter arose from non-living material is called spontaneous generation. The idea of maggots coming spontaneously to life out of decaying meat was successfully challenged in 1668 by Italian biologist Francesco Redi. When he covered the meat with gauze to prevent flies from laying their eggs on it, no maggots appeared in the meat. (The maggots are actually the larvae which hatch from flies' eggs.)

A hundred and fifty years ago, Frenchman Louis Pasteur confirmed this result, proving once and for all that spontaneous generation doesn't happen. So there's no empirical evidence for life arising without the necessity for the existence of a life-giving God. There's no such thing as a simple cell. The so-called simplest bacterial cell is still much more complex than anything which we humans have ever made, with a hundred thousand million atoms. The gulf between this and anything non-living is as vast and absolute as anyone could care to imagine. Antony Flew, a famously converted British atheist, concluded from the microscopic world of the cell that the almost unbelievable complexity of the arrangements which are needed to produce life shows that intelligence must have been involved.

But you may vaguely remember a headline that once claimed life had been artificially created in the laboratory (the work of Craig Venter). Headlines are, however, often misleading. This is what really happened: just as computers use a computer code made up of programmed instructions, the cells in our body use the genetic code. In other words, cells process information in a similar way to computers. They do this in order to make proteins and other cell bits. The living cell is like an incredibly powerful computer. What was done in the lab experiment was the equivalent of making a careful copy of one version of Microsoft Windows, and turning to another computer which had previously been using a different version of Microsoft Windows and loading instead this new copy version onto it, so that when we next switch it on, that computer can now do some things it couldn't do before. But this process doesn't involve developing a totally new brand of software nor does it involve building computer hardware that didn't exist previously. It used a software design and a computer which already existed – which means the headline about life having been created in the laboratory was very misleading.

We said cells are like computers, and most of the workings of the cell are best described not in terms of material stuff – which we might call the hardware - but in terms of information or software. Something else we can deduce from that is that trying to make life by just mixing chemicals in a tank or test tube – as in some previous famous laboratory experiments – is like soldering switches and wires in an attempt to produce Microsoft Windows. That's confusing hardware with software. Which leaves scientists (e.g. Paul Davies) to this very day still puzzling over how life could have arisen from non-living chemicals. The key question is how did the hardware of non-living molecules ever manage to write its own software?

The origin of life is one of the great outstanding mysteries of science. Scientists have no agreed theory of the origin of life – plenty of scenarios, conjectures and just-so stories, but nothing with solid experimental support. Well-known American Atheist philosopher, Thomas Nagel asked, "Given what is known about the chemical basis of biology and genetics, what is the likelihood that self-reproducing life forms should have come into existence spontaneously on the early earth, solely through the operation of the laws of physics and chemistry?" The chance that higher life forms might have emerged through evolutionary processes has been said (by Sir Fred Hoyle) to be comparable with the chance that a tornado sweeping through a junk yard might assemble a Boeing 747 from the material found there. Once we see, however, that the probability of life originating at random is so utterly tiny as to make it absurd, then it becomes sensible to think that the highly favourable properties of physics, on which life depends, are in every respect deliberate. He also said that the fossil evidence of the simplest bacterial cells we can find shows that we cannot reach back to evidence of any simple beginning.

While the subject of the origin of life is hardly mentioned in Darwin's published writings, the following quote (from a letter to his botanist friend Joseph Hooker) gives us an inkling of his thoughts on the subject at that time. Darwin said: "If (and oh! what a big if!) we could conceive in some warm little pond, with all sorts of ammonia and phosphoric salts, light, heat, electricity present, that a protein compound was chemically formed, ready to undergo still more complex changes ..." Others in the early twentieth century developed the idea that chemical reactions on the early Earth could have led to the production of a "primordial soup" in which the required building blocks for life would have been present. But in reality, and with updated information available to us now, there's not a shred of objective evidence to support the idea that life began in any kind of warm pond of chemicals here on the Earth. In fact, one specialist researcher (Michael Denton) has said that considering the way the (prebiotic) soup is referred to in so many discussions of the origin of life as an already established reality, it comes as something of a shock to realize that there is absolutely no positive evidence for its existence.

In 1953, a famous experiment in which electrical discharges were passed through a mixture of gases attempted to recreate the conditions of a thunderstorm on the primitive Earth. Some chemicals basic to life were produced, but both the starting point and the end result are now considered to be unfit for purpose. What's more, in the same year, Crick and Watson published their structure for DNA. This would turn out to be the first step in bringing to light the wonderful molecular basis of life. Only an incredibly intelligent designer could account for these information systems in living things. One of those to unlock the secrets of DNA (Francis Crick) has conceded that "Biologists must constantly keep in mind that what they see was not designed, but rather evolved." Now, doesn't that sound as if he's denying the undeniable? He'd found clear evidence for design, sufficient to convert a hardened atheist, as we said.

Professor Paul Davies sums it up, "How did stupid atoms spontaneously write their own software … ? Nobody knows … there is no known law of physics able to create information from nothing." In fact, in quite recent times, information has come to be thought of as a third fundamental quantity. None less than Einstein declared that symbols, meaning and information could never have arisen from matter or stuff. The DNA code must be explained, for how can a coded information storage system come about without intelligent design? But also, the incredible machinery that reads the information and creates the components of life from that information has to be explained as well.

Let's again quote former hard-nosed British atheist philosopher Antony Flew who abandoned his atheism because of the growing evidence for such design in living things. He said, "It now seems to me that the findings of more than fifty years of DNA research have provided materials for a new and enormously powerful argument to design." This research "has shown, by the almost unbelievable complexity of the arrangements which are needed to produce (life), that intelligence must have been involved." As the scientific knowledge of life grows, the prospects of a purely natural explanation for life's origin recede into the distance. The origin of life is definitely another miracle. As the Apostle Paul told his audience at Athens: *"In him* [God] *we live and move and have our being."* The origin of life demands a *super*-intelligent cause, such as the Creator-God revealed in the Bible. *"In the beginning God created the heavens and the earth"* (Genesis 1:1).

4

The Origin of Biodiversity

There are at least five major times when those who don't believe in God are forced instead to believe in 'magic' in the sense of believing in events without any sufficient explanation or cause for those events – that could therefore be styled as 'miraculous' events. So far, we've looked at the origin of the universe, the origin of stars in particular and the origin of life itself. Let's now think about something we hear a lot about today. I'm referring to biodiversity, that is the diversity of life, and how it might have come about.

The difference in the genetic makeup (genomes) of humans and chimps was once said to be only 1%, but it's now estimated as much higher than that, perhaps showing a 20% difference or even a 30% difference, depending on how you measure it. Diversity of life on our planet is genuinely a huge problem for some theories of origins. How did a microbe change itself into every living thing on earth, ranging from earwigs to elephants, and from mites to mango trees? Mutations combined with natural selection have been said to explain this diversity of life.

However, with our modern knowledge of living things, this would now appear more and more hopeless as an explanation.

But, of course, please don't take my word for that. In July 2008, 16 high-profile evolutionists met, by invitation, in Altenburg, Austria. They'd come together because they realized that mutations and natural selection did not explain the diversity of life, and so they'd come together to discuss what for them was a crisis. The only consensus they could reach was that there is a major problem in their Godless understanding of the origin of biodiversity or the diversity of living things. One of them put it this way:

> "[Another] question is about the sources of variation in the evolutionary process that was set in motion once life began: in the available geological time since the first life forms appeared on earth, what is the likelihood that, as a result of physical accident, a sequence of viable genetic mutations should have occurred that was sufficient to permit natural selection to produce the organisms that actually exist?"

Obviously, that's a very basic question, one being asked in despair by highly informed specialists. The recent publication of the actual human and chimp DNA sequences finally made possible a more realistic comparison than the earlier ones that previously estimated there was only a genetic difference of about 1%. And yet the 1% myth is still being perpetuated, for example in a 2012 *Science* journal. Illustrating how wrong this figure of a 1% difference is, in that same year of 2012 other scientists reviewed the published studies comparing human and chimp

DNA. When all the DNA is taken into account, and not just pre-selected parts, they found "it is safe to conclude that human-chimp genome similarity is not more than about 87% identical, and possibly not higher than 81%" (Drs Jeffrey Tomkins and Jerry Bergman). In other words, forget 1% - the differences are possibly greater than 19%. Indeed, one of the specialists involved in that same study made his own thorough comparison and found the difference to be about 30%.

It's useful to have some idea of what's going on here. Comparing the genetic make-up of chimps and humans involves making assumptions, such as about the importance of various parts of the DNA. For example, what do you do with human genes that are absent from chimps and vice versa? The tendency has been to ignore them and only compare the similar genes. There again, many comparisons have involved only the genes involved in the production of proteins (which is only 1.2% of the DNA – many of these are indeed quite similar). But this assumes that the rest of the DNA is "not important" or might even be regarded as 'junk.' However, it's now becoming realized that almost all, if not all, DNA probably has a function. This is one major reason why earlier studies had over-emphasised the similarity between chimps and humans. We humans are certainly not 99% identical with chimps; nothing like it.

In any case, let's realize that there's actually a much more basic question: What does any percentage of similarity prove anyway? Does it indicate common ancestry or does it suggest common design? The answer to that is going to depend on the researcher's worldview. And, of course, results of studies are always interpreted in accordance with the framework of the experimenter. In understanding the implications of the data here, we're not dealing with hard science that can be shown by experiments; but only interpretations based on different worldviews.

What we can all agree on is this: the larger the actual genetic difference between apes and humans, the bigger the problem in trying to explain this in terms of time and chance alone. And as our knowledge grows that gap is definitely growing. And yet the myth of similarity persists. The reason for this, as we've hinted, would not appear to be scientific but more to do with the researcher's underlying worldview. The myth of similarity will tend to be held onto by those who look to support the claim that humans have no special place in the world – and even that chimps should be granted human rights.

The recent re-evaluation of what's now thought to be the real position is much more consistent with humans having been created quite separately from the animals – which agrees with the New Testament of the Bible, where the Apostle Paul says: *"All flesh is not the same flesh, but there is one flesh of mankind, another flesh of animals, another flesh of birds, and another of fish"* (1 Corinthians 15:39). A straightforward reading (but confirmed by experts) of the opening chapters of Genesis leaves no doubt that we're engaging with Hebrew narrative and not Hebrew in its poetry form. The Bible's first book tells us plainly that Adam was not made from, nor did he come from, any pre-existing living creatures. Rather, it actually says that he was made (directly) from the dust. Genesis 2:7 says *"And the LORD God formed man of the dust of the ground, and breathed into his nostrils the breath of life; and man became a living soul."*

In this way, man is made in the image of God and is different from the animals (Genesis 1:27; 1 Corinthians 11:7). Opinions and speculations abound, of course, but if we take the Bible at all seriously, surely we'd want to weigh the precise meaning of man being formed from the dust of the ground alongside Genesis 3:19 which states, *"Till you return to the ground, Because from it you were taken; For you are dust, And to dust you shall return."* Our decay back to dust at death is not a poetic description but is sober reality. This leaves us with no choice over how to understand the Bible's meaning about human origins. The texts in Genesis 2:7 and 3:19, taken together, plainly mean Adam was made from actual dust in the first place, and not from a pre-existing creature.

God made the first man from dust (Genesis 2:7) and the first woman from his rib (Genesis 2:22), not from any ape-like creature. And humans, unlike other creatures, were made in the image of God (Genesis 1:26,27), as a special creation. This image was not lost but was marred when our first parents rebelled against God their creator, as we can read in the Bible narrative of Genesis chapter 3. According to the Bible's account, God made humans with a special purpose both for now and in eternity. Without God in the frame, there's no sufficient explanation or cause for the diversity of life. Biodiversity becomes an unexplained miracle. In fact, more than one. Every basic type of life form is a miracle!

And we should register the undisputed fact that buried deep down in the record of rock layers covering our planet, there's a point (known as the Great Unconformity) where all major types of all lifeforms are 'suddenly' represented. This is universally recognised as the most important surface in the geological record (where the so-called "Cambrian explosion" of all those diverse lifeforms being suddenly represented seemingly at one time flies in the face of Godless theories). Genesis 1 tells us that God, the all-powerful, all-knowing Creator, made the various kinds of life to reproduce "after their kind." Here is a sufficient cause, but even the description of the nature of living things to reproduce according to each kind has been confirmed with every witnessed reproductive event (billions of humans alone), and also in the fossil record where the so-called "missing links" are – as the name says – missing.

Again we ask - why do intelligent people resort to believing in magic—uncaused events—at so many points? By not believing in God they have put themselves into an irrational philosophical corner. Romans 1:21 in the Bible says that when people deny that the Creator-God exists, they end up with "futile thinking.' Geneticist Richard Lewontin admits that when leaving God out of the picture, those who take the side of a purely natural worldview do so 'in spite of the patent absurdity of some of its constructs.' This very much includes belief in things for which we have no evidence and that are contrary to basic logic.

5

The Origin of Mind and Morality

A fig tree produces figs, not apples. That seems obvious. It's also true that physics and chemistry produce physical and chemical outcomes. However, mind and morality are not just matters of physics and chemistry. Sure, creatures that are physical and chemical have mind and morality, but how did such non-material things arise from the material? This is a serious problem for those who believe only in time and chance, as the more candid atheists admit.

The origin of mind and morality from energy and atoms has long been a problem for them – in fact, it's a major theme of philosopher Thomas Nagel's book, *Mind and Cosmos*. Atheists have no sufficient cause to explain the existence of mind and morality – it's as if magic just happens! But someone may say: "Morality, at the end of the day, just boils down to doing to others what you'd like them to do to you – nothing more than that." OK, that's a good start, but I think I've heard that before somewhere. Indeed I have; it's found in the biblical teachings of Jesus in Matthew 7:12.

But tell me, if we're only here because of some cosmic chemical accident then why should one chemical accident even care about another? And yet we do. There are loved ones you care about, and it's the same for me. Ah, but you come back and say: "Morality is just an electro-chemical phenomenon in the brain." Really? Chemicals do what chemicals do - nothing morally right about it. I once heard someone reply: "I've got chemistry going on in my stomach, but I'm not relying on my indigestion to set my moral compass." Someone else, however, might say that a sense of morality is built up from societal conventions. Well, Nazi Germany set its societal conventions, and I hope you don't think that was just as valid. Again, others may say: morality is just down to parental brainwashing. That does seem rather short-sighted, doesn't it? For we need to ask: "Where did your parents get their sense of right and wrong from?" Let's think for a moment about our conscience. Here's what Paul has to say in the Bible:

> *"For when Gentiles who do not have the Law do instinctively the things of the Law, these, not having the Law, are a law to themselves, in that they show the work of the Law written in their hearts, their conscience bearing witness and their thoughts alternately accusing or else defending them, on the day when, according to my gospel, God will judge the secrets of men through Christ Jesus"* (Romans 2:14-16).

Many everyday expressions in the western world have come from the Bible in its King James Version form. And what we've just read contains an example – when we read the words: *"a law to themselves."* Interestingly, when we hear people being accused of being a law to themselves, it seems to be generally implying that they're rebellious and out of control. But that's not how the Bible uses it here. In fact, it's the very opposite! Paul was saying that it was to the Jews that the Law with its Ten Commandments was given. These commands weren't formally given to non-Jews or Gentiles. But even so, when Gentiles end up doing, by instinct, the very things which the Law commands, then they're demonstrating that the same Law has in fact been written on all of our hearts. So it's correct behaviour that's evidence of a hidden law – written, not on external stone tables – but actually inside us on the tables of human hearts. And will you notice please that Paul describes it as "the Law" - it's God's Law. This Law, written on human hearts, is the basis for our conscience. And it's this that shows that we're moral beings.

It was Immanuel Kant, the 18th century German philosopher, who said "Two things fill the mind with ever new and increasing wonder and awe: the starry heavens above me and the moral law within me." From the atheistic point of view, apart from their social consequences, there's really nothing basically wrong with many socially unacceptable things – things like when a man rapes a woman. Because without God there isn't any absolute standard of right and wrong which imposes itself on our conscience. Without God, morality becomes nothing more than a matter of personal taste or social conditioning. This is exactly the point many people have pressed on me in conversations about faith when, as mentioned before, they try to tell me that our attitude to something like rape basically only comes down to what our parents and society have taught us. You've got to then ask them where their parents got their values from ... and where their grandparents got theirs from ... and so on all the way back to the first ever humans. And at that point it's a problem. For blind forces of nature can't explain the origin of any absolute morality.

The late J.L. Mackie of Oxford University, one of the most influential atheists of our time, admitted, "If ... there ... are objective values, they make the existence of a god more probable than it would have been without them ... [there is, he said] ... a defensible argument from morality to the existence of a god. ..." Notice his words: "a defensible argument." On the other hand, Paul, in Romans, has just said atheists have no defence for their claim that there is no God (Romans 1:20; 2:1). So Paul locked horns with the atheists, and we're faced with a clear-cut choice and it's one we can easily put to the test. Here it is. On the one hand, the Word of God says objective moral values really do exist, and deep down we all know it; on the other hand, atheism says objective, absolute moral values don't exist – while admitting that if they did exist, that would give the game away.

Richard Dawkins agrees that rape is wrong but concedes that in arriving at that view his value judgement is every bit as arbitrary as the fact we've evolved 5 fingers rather than 6. We quote professors Mackie and Dawkins only so as to give assurance that atheists as well as Christians agree on this as a fair test. It's fair and accurate to judge the question of God's existence based on judging the question of the existence or otherwise of objective, absolute moral values.

So then, suppose you take a group of people and ask each of them

"Do you like vegetables?" Some will say "I like vegetables," others will say "I don't like vegetables." And that's fine. It's a subjective thing, a matter of personal taste. But what if instead of asking the question "Do you like vegetables?" we were to ask "Is it okay to torture children for fun?" You'll surely agree that we've crossed a boundary line. You wouldn't expect the same group of reasonable people whose personal tastes on vegetables varied, to show the same spread of opinion on this question, would you? But why not? Because – I submit – this is no longer a subjective matter of personal taste, we've moved on to an altogether different matter: one that's an objective matter of right and wrong.

One famous writer (C. S. Lewis) illustrates the difference by making this comparison, he said: "The reason my idea of New York city can be truer than yours is because New York is a real place existing apart from what either of us thinks." On the other hand, if we were trying to compare ideas about some imaginary city, then neither idea could be truer than the other because there's no basis for any comparison." Our first example about vegetables was like that, but returning to our second example of torturing children, the reason why we'd agree that one reaction is truer than the other is because a real standard of absolute morality exists apart from whatever happen to be our own personal tastes and preferences. Torturing children for fun is not a morally neutral act – it's an outrageous moral abomination. It wouldn't matter in which culture we performed the experiment. We've identified a consensus on morality which transcends culture.

Actions like rape, torture, child abuse, and so forth, aren't just socially unacceptable behaviour. They're moral abominations: things which are absolutely wrong. Similarly, love, equality, generosity, and self-sacrifice are really good. And the point is this: **if objective values cannot exist without God, but we find that they do exist, then it logically follows that God also exists.**

II

The Success of the 'God Hypothesis'

It predicts:
6 The Universe's Origin Cannot Be Explained in Purely Material Terms
7 There Should be a Principle of Rationality Underlying the Universe
8 Laws are Best Explained by a Law-giver
9 The Essence of Life Resides Not in Chemistry But in (Organised) Information
10 There Should be Irreducibly Complex Design Features
11 Time Had a Beginning

6

The Universe's Origin Cannot Be Explained in Purely Material Terms

In the first part of this book, we've reviewed five major 'gaps' in scientific knowledge. These we've seen are the failures to explain the origin of the universe, the origin of stars, the origin of life, the origin of biodiversity, and the origin of morality. Of course, speculations are made as to a universe creating itself out of nothing, the notion of so-called "dark matter," a warm pond with primordial chemicals etc. But when we listen carefully to specialists at the top of their game, at times we've heard the candid acknowledgement that mystery remains, a mystery we've labelled "magic." That's for the reason that if the existence of a supernatural designer is ruled out from the start, no other convincing explanation remains.

To escape this predicament, we've turned back to the famous opening lines of the Bible: "*In the beginning God created the heavens and the earth*" (Genesis 1:1). We've stated that this isn't magic, because the eternal and omnipotent God is a *sufficient cause* for the universe. He can exist eternally (without a beginning) because he's not a material being. Despite having been compiled three and a half thousand years ago, this is still the most up-to-date account of origins we have. That does seem an extraordinary claim, so let's put it to the test. A modern scientific type of approach we could apply here (one that Professor Edgar Andrews advocates in his book 'Who Made God?') is to create a hypothesis and then ask: "If that's true, what predictions would it make?" Then we observe the evidence available to assess the accuracy or otherwise of those predictions. Have they come to pass or have they failed?

So, let our hypothesis be simply this: that the God of the Bible exists and that in the beginning he created the heavens and the earth. Supposing that's true. what would it lead us to expect? In the second part of this book, I want to propose six major things that would be predicted if we took our stand on the first ten words of the Bible. Before doing that, and perhaps to reassure some of the credibility of this whole approach, let's first hear from a famous scientist.

Arno Penzias, a Nobel Prize-winning scientist who co-discovered cosmic background radiation, reacted with the statement when asked about his view of origins: "The best data we have are exactly what I would have predicted, had I nothing to go on but the five Books of Moses, the Psalms, the Bible as a whole" (cited by Meyer on p.243 of *The Return of the God Hypothesis*). How is it that this Nobel Prize-winner is able to say this? Well, let's now turn to some predictions of what we're styling as our "God-hypothesis." And the first is:

1. **That the origin of the material universe should NOT be able to be explained in purely material terms.**

The first prediction of the God-hypothesis is underlined in the New Testament: *"By faith we understand that the world has been created by the word of God so that what is seen has not been made out of things that are visible"* (Hebrews 11:3). The very first comment must be that here we are now talking about a beginning. That has not always been the view of the scientific establishment. But the work of Penzias, whom we've just mentioned, is generally viewed as having settled the question in favour of our universe having a beginning. That in itself, of course, is a satisfied prediction of the biblical God-hypothesis that agrees with the Bible's very first verse.

The acceptance of a beginning, however, means there was an eternity when the space-time universe as yet did not exist, and so time itself did not exist (time being measured by changes in energy). Turning now to the universe as a whole, the prevailing scientific consensus is that when we work the mathematical descriptions of the universe backwards in time, Einstein's famous equation describing the law of gravity condenses everything backwards in time to a hot super dense point. This is taken as the starting point for the subsequent expansion and development of the universe. That super dense point is strikingly described as a "singularity" because of the fact that, at that point, the known laws of science or physics break down. That breakdown of the laws of science at the point of origin does mean that we are left without any scientific explanation, at least in terms of the laws of science as they are known to us today.

What then did it begin from and what caused it to begin? Ultimately, it can't be explained by somehow having come from the same sort of stuff as our present universe, because then that earlier matter or energy in turn would have required a beginning too, just further back in time – and that would also need to be explained. That's what we mean when we say that modern science has not explained the origin of all things in purely material terms. Genesis chapter 1 repeatedly uses the phrase *"And God said."* The person whom the Bible reveals to us as Jesus Christ (Colossians 1:16; John 1:1-3) is later identified as the agent of creation. The Bible offers us many proofs that Jesus Christ is fully God and fully man. Nothing else satisfies all the facts. On earth, by merely speaking, the God-man, Jesus of Nazareth, performed wonders instantly in the natural world. His word alone was enough to heal the paralyzed and tormented; and to raise the dead (Matthew 8:8,13; John 11:43). And there was an immediate response to it, such that we read that the wind and the waves immediately obey the voice of Christ (Matthew 8:27).

Genesis, and the Bible as a whole, knows of no known process being used in creation, only the word and will of God. The scientific laws we can discover (by "thinking God's thoughts after him," as Kepler said) govern how the completed universe _continues_ to operate. Atheistic scientists like Richard Dawkins admit that science has no "strongly satisfying" explanation for why the universe appears to have been fine-tuned with the precise conditions ideally suited to life as we know it, but he urges his readers (*The God Delusion*, pp.157,158) "not to give up hope" in "some kind of multiverse theory." This refers to the totally speculative idea that a trillion trillion parallel universes exist simply to explain the remote chance of this one being exactly as it is. In this unpublicized section of his best-selling book, Dawkins appeals to his readers not to give up hope in the discovery of some new scientific theory that will one day save atheism! On the other hand, the best-selling book that is the Bible says: *"that which is known about God is evident ... for God made it evident ... for since the creation of the world His invisible attributes ... have been clearly seen ... through what has been made ... [but] they did not honour Him as God ... but they became futile in their speculations"* (Romans 1:19-21).

Summing up, the problem for physics is it doesn't have a satisfying explanation other than desperately hoping in some multiverse theory. The problem for chemistry is that it alone cannot explain information. A printed page with meaningful words cannot be distinguished by any chemical analysis alone from a printed page using the exact same letters but with them all scrambled up. The problem for biology is that it cannot back to a time when there was a simple beginning. Even the smallest self-reproducing cells are very sophisticated. And the genetic code was already there – right from the start of life, the fundamental biochemical problems were already solved. The problem for palaeontology or the study of fossils is that there was a sudden unprecedented explosion of myriads of life-forms (at the Cambrian boundary). The late Stephen Hawking can do no better than defy basic logic when he said: "Because there is a law like gravity, the universe can and will create itself from nothing ..." (Hawking and Mlodinow, *The Grand Design*, 2010, p.180.)

Overall, we can sum up by saying the first prediction of the God

hypothesis is satisfied. The origin of the material universe has not been explained in purely material terms. It is widely recognized that there has to be more than mass and energy. The clear implication is that symbols, information and language represent a category of reality distinct from matter and energy. And its origin is one of the profound questions about the world. That means there are, in fact, three fundamental quantities: mass and energy, but also information. Einstein said he could identify no means by which matter could give meaning to symbols. That means that something that's now recognised as a fundamental quantity of our universe cannot be explained in purely material terms. The DNA code of all life-forms is an example of information, which, like any other information, cannot arise from anything material, but requires an intelligent sender. This is nothing other than the supernatural intelligence whom the Bible introduces to us as the Judeo-Christian God.

7

There Should be a Principle of Rationality Underlying the Universe

We've already thought about scientific speculations and interpretations of evidence that come from looking at things from a particular worldview. And that worldview was one that said 'Nature' is all there is. We saw that reasoning from that starting point doesn't allow us to reach any adequate explanation for the origin of the universe, of its stars, of life on this planet, of its diversity, nor of how morality arose. We've now switched to an alternative worldview: one which holds that the God of the Bible exists as the creator of the universe. Our approach now is to create a hypothesis: that the God of the Bible exists. We're asking: "What would be the predictions of that hypothesis?"

Already, we've talked about how it should predict that we should not be able to find an adequate material or natural explanation for how the universe began. And neither can we, as we saw in the last chapter. **The second prediction of what we're calling "the God-hypothesis" is that there should be a principle of rationality underlying the entire universe.** Commonly, there's talk about the so-called "laws of nature," although in a worldview that acknowledges God as creator, we might be better calling these "the thoughts of God." Devout scientists once believed they were simply thinking God's thoughts after him when they studied the workings of the universe. It was those thoughts they tried to express, at least approximately, with the laws of science. They, and we today, can do this, we will now contend, because we are created in the image of God. This fact enables us to consider its beautiful symmetries and have an aesthetic appreciation of them (Ecclesiastes 3:11).

Albert Einstein once complained "in view of such harmony in the cosmos which I, with my limited human mind am able to recognise, there are yet people who say there is no God ..." So, to repeat, the second prediction of the God-hypothesis is that there should be a principle of rationality underlying the entire universe. And straightaway we note that Einstein, whom we've just quoted helps us. He's on record as saying: "The most incomprehensible thing about the universe is that it's comprehensible." Scientist Dr Paul Davies had this to say in his 1995 Templeton Prize Address: "Even the most atheistic scientist accepts as an act of faith that the universe is not absurd, that there is a rational basis to physical existence manifested as a law-like order in nature that is at least in part comprehensible to us. So science can proceed only if the scientist adopts an essentially theological worldview."

Now that's really remarkable. And Professor Sir John Polkinghorne wrote, "Science does not explain the mathematical intelligibility of the physical world, for it is part of science's founding faith that this is so ..." for the simple reason that you cannot begin to do physics without believing in that intelligibility. On what evidence, therefore, do scientists base their faith in the rational intelligibility of the universe, which allows them to do science? How can it be that a mathematical equation thought up in the mind of a scientist can correspond to the workings of the universe?

The Nobel Prize-winning physicist Eugene Wigner once wrote a famous paper entitled, *"The unreasonable effectiveness of mathematics in the natural sciences."* But it's only unreasonable from an atheistic perspective. From the biblical point of view, it resonates perfectly with the statements: *"In the beginning was the Word ... and the Word was God ... All things came to be through him"* (John 1:1,3). Notice that it says "all things": that includes both the material universe around us and our conscious mind within. Let's come back to our earlier question. What other possible reason can there be for how what goes on in our tiny heads can give us anything near a true account of reality?

Professor John Lennox says: "Sometimes, when in conversation with my fellow scientists, I ask them 'What do you do science with?' 'My mind,' say some, and others, who hold the view that the mind is the brain, say, 'My brain.' 'Tell me about your brain? How does it come to exist?' 'By means of natural, mindless, unguided processes.' 'Why, then, do you trust it?' I ask. 'If you thought that your computer was the end product of mindless unguided processes, would you trust it?' 'Not in a million years,' comes the reply. 'You clearly have a problem then.' After a pregnant pause they sometimes ask me where I got this argument—they find the answer rather surprising: Charles Darwin. He wrote: "... with me the horrid doubt always arises whether the convictions of man's mind, which has been developed from the mind of the lower animals, are of any value or at all trustworthy."'

To take the obvious logic of this statement further, physicist John Polkinghorne says that if you reduce mental events to physics and chemistry you destroy meaning. How? For thought is replaced by electrochemical events firing off between our brain cells. Two such events cannot confront each other in rational discourse. They are neither right nor wrong—they simply happen. Quite frankly that can't be right and none of us believe it to be so. Polkinghorne is a Christian, but some well-known atheists see the problem as well. When we examine the laws of nature (e.g., the Law of Gravity), we quickly discover that they're based on mathematics and model how God has chosen – ordinarily – to govern the universe ...

> *"The fact that nature can be described mathematically has been a continuing surprise to those who cannot think beyond their presuppositions of materialistic naturalism. They have difficulty explaining why there is a connection between physical reality and abstract mathematics. The fact that there is, indicates that the universe is more than the sum of its parts and is the product of intelligent thought... the existence of mathematics declares to [humanity] that God is behind the order in the universe. We can count and perform mathematical calculations because we are image-bearers of God (Genesis 1:26–27), and can think God's thoughts after Him.* (James R. Hughes, Mathematics, from the mind of God, CMI).

The existence of counting and mathematics is evidence that the universe was created by an intelligent designer—the God of the Bible. The laws of mathematics (e.g., commutative, associative, and distributive) come from God's mind. He is the ultimate lawgiver. If mathematics is purely an invention of human minds, then it's a challenge to explain the correspondence between a mathematical equation and what happens in the natural realm. This connection between physical reality and abstract mathematics is one that's always personally fascinated me and led to my own career in science before God called me to other things. I would agree with those who claim that mathematics is more than an abstraction of physical reality. There's a reality about what lies behind the symbols and their operations – maybe an even deeper reality than the physical realities themselves – and one which permits them to materialise.

Sir Roger Penrose is someone who has shared awards with Stephen Hawking. It's his mathematics that described the formation of black holes. When he was talking about a mathematical object (something known as "the Mandelbrot set"[1]), he described it as mathematical experimentation to discover real entities that exist. This is about using mathematics to discover what's "out there," as opposed to thinking of mathematics purely as a human invention. Mathematical experimentation can produce beautiful patterns of deeply hidden realities; a trace of a fundamental reality underlying what the symbols represent and the operations between their pre-existing realities.

Summing up, the connection between physical reality and abstract mathematics shows the universe is the product of intelligent thought - the existence of mathematics points to the God who is behind the order that's found in the universe. It implies there's a deeper mystery than what's visible to us, meaning that we cannot deduce all that's true from what we already know. Truth is just "out there" somewhere. And mathematics tells us (Kurt Godel's incompleteness theorem[2]) that based on what we know, there will always be propositions or statements that we cannot decide upon as to whether they are true or not. Truth is out there, unreachable by the force of logic. Truth comes by divine revelation. Jesus Christ said *"I am the way, the truth and the life"* (John 14:6).

Footnotes:

1. The Mandelbrot set is a geometric form of awesome beauty generated by plugging values for z into $F(z) = z^2 + c$ (where c is a numerical constant). Each answer is fed back in repeatedly as a new value of z and so it's applied successively. When the results are graphed, the Mandelbrot set of beautiful geometric form materialises which is an object possessing self-similarity at different scales within itself.
2. A Cretan says: "All Cretans are liars" (Titus 1:12). Let S be the statement: "All Cretans are liars." If S is true, then what the Cretan says (i.e. S) is false. Also, if S is false, then S is true. This is, in effect, an example of what Kurt Godel's Incompleteness Theorem says - namely that, based on what we know, there will also be statements (e.g. S) that we cannot work out as to whether they are true or false. Divine revelation is required (see v.13 ... S is in fact true).

8

Laws are Best Explained by a Law-giver

In taking God's existence as a working hypothesis and testing the predictions of such a "God-hypothesis," we'd expect there to be no realistic scientific way of explaining the beginning of the universe in purely natural terms – and that's what we find. We'd also expect the universe to be rational, not random – and once again, that's what we observe, and what's more, we also find our own rationality to be a match for it.

Now we want to look at a third prediction based on the hypothesis that God exists and created the universe. And that's the expectation **that the laws that govern the workings of the universe are best explained by the existence of a lawgiver**. Let's explore that. What's meant by laws of nature? The aim of science seems to be to discover them. But who, or what, enforces the law? Does some agent "make" a cannonball follow the curve that's known as a parabola? Who gave the law that governs that? Most threw out the idea of a Divine Lawgiver in the 19th century.

To see how that came about, let's rewind. During the 14th and

16th centuries in Europe, there had been a movement known as the Renaissance. As the name suggests it was a revival of interest in literature generally, and this included the study of the Bible in its original languages, but also as translated into European languages such as German and English. It was a time when all kinds of learning flourished, and it was the time when the foundations of modern science were laid too. And there was a definite connection between scientific progress and the renewed interest in the Bible at that time. The return to the literal approach to biblical truth at this time fuelled advances in science. God-fearing scientists looked for law in nature because of their belief in the existence of a Law-giver: he being the Bible's author. When they found that law in nature, modern science was born. This was because it seemed to them that the existence of all laws – be they of nature, conscience or society – should best be explained by a supernatural law-giver; and that the laws of nature are the normal providential expression of God's moment-by-moment will (which can at times be overridden by a miraculous expression of the same).

So much then for the European Renaissance. It was followed by the so-called "Enlightenment" of the 17th to 19th centuries. In 1785, Scottish geologist James Hutton ruled out of court biblical explanations for the history of our planet. He decided, simply as a given, that the present must be the key to the past. Others built on his ideas, and even declared that their goal was to free science from Moses. That was how the 18th century ended, and things were set to get no better in the nineteenth. In the first half of the 19th century, an attitude to the Bible known as "higher criticism" swept through German universities, spreading doubts about the Bible. This was an approach, a way of thinking, that questioned the Bible's authority. It opened the door for what was to follow in the second half of the 19th century. Godless speculation built on this scepticism.

In 1859, Darwin's Origin of Species rewrote biblical history as not being "his story" – that's God's story - but simply the tale of our own accidental and improbable arrival. In 1900, the German philosopher Nietzsche, died but only after first having declared God to have predeceased him – God was dead, he said, as a philosophical idea. It was no coincidence that the 20th century that followed became the bloodiest in modern times, because in it accountability to any supernatural authority was set aside. The 64-million dollar question, as they say, is which worldview is correct? Is it the biblical worldview of the Renaissance or the sceptical worldview of the Enlightenment? History is witness to the fact that it was the former, biblical worldview that gave birth to modern science. Galileo, Isaac Newton, Kepler, Kelvin and many, many more were all devout believers in God. In fact, around 70% of scientific Nobel-prizewinners during the 20th century believed in God. That fact alone ought to dispel any myth that theism is only fit for persons who are weak in the head. Intellect is not at all the issue when it comes to matters of faith.

The worldview of the Renaissance is essentially the same as our "God-hypothesis." And the founders of modern science discovered the laws of science because they were predisposed to belief in a Law-giver, the creator God of the Bible. The more sceptical stance that came in with the Enlightenment permits the question: are the laws of nature simply useful generalizations, whose strength is measured by their explanatory power or predictive potential within our best theories? Is the basis for the laws of nature truly "out there" or is it just "in our heads"?

Scientific realists hold to the belief that the laws of nature are really "out there" in the world, and that science only "discovers" them. And the only basis for laws of nature that are truly "out there" – and not just "in our heads" – is belief in a personal, rational, consistent, freely-acting, transcendent, powerful God as described in the Bible. Our own rationality presupposes a rational source. Why would particles become scientists? Why would matter seek understanding? The human propensity to find laws of nature implies a Lawgiver who created that propensity in us. The Divine Lawgiver, therefore, is not a metaphor, nor a placeholder for ignorance; he is a logical necessity for science.

It is true that apart from God's works we could think no rational thoughts; people can think certain rational thoughts precisely because God has endowed his creation with rationality; it reflects his very nature. Without this in-built logic or rationality it would not be possible to live. And with it, no one has any excuse! Reflecting on the writings of the great 18th century Christian apologist Jonathan Edwards, Martin Murphy wrote, "The law of non-contradiction, the law of causality, and the basic reliability of sense perception are three components necessary to communicate truth." These laws of logic are embedded in the created order, and so they are revealed in the creation. Such logic is "built-in" - part of the way in which the creation reveals the attributes of God (Romans 1:19,20,25). Expressed in other terms, this gives us three tests for truth, and they are: logical consistency, empirical adequacy, and experiential relevance.

Logical consistency satisfies the law of non-contradiction: something cannot be both true and not true under the same circumstances. It seeks to show that the worldview in question makes sense within itself. It asks: is it logical? The sceptical worldview fails this test. If the universe created itself, then it must have both existed and not existed at the same time. It had to exist to do the creating, and not exist in order to be created. Similar problems exist if we come into being from non-being, come into life from non-life. And how can we maintain morality coming from non-morality? Atheists borrow concepts of ethics, value and purpose from another worldview because atheism cannot logically account for it. But in the worldview of the God-hypothesis, basic doctrines like God existing, the Incarnation, the Resurrection, and even the Trinity are logically consistent. That's not to say that we can comprehend the complexity of a thing, but there has to be no apparent logical fallacy in them. Every other worldview is logically inconsistent.

The test of empirical adequacy asks if we can verify facts empirically. In other words, does it fit the facts of reality. Or again, is it factual? Does it correspond to the real world? Proposed truth claims must have explanatory power: that is, be able to give account for our experience of the world. For instance, a worldview can be tested by its ability to explain questions like the origin of the universe – and that's what we're doing with the God-hypothesis. If a worldview isn't able to justify what it's claiming, by any cause or effect, it might as well be claiming anything it wants. This would be most specifically applied to the Christian claims of Jesus. When we look at Jesus we see that he was a real man who existed in history, is attested to by the Bible and by non-Biblical sources, has eye-witness testimony, and all located within 1st century history. If we want to look into the claims of the Christian worldview, all we have to is historically test the claims of the New Testament with the standard methods and draw our conclusion based on what we find.

Experiential relevance is the test that asks how this makes sense and how it relates to my life. In short, is this claim livable? Does it work in real life? Some views only sound good on paper. For the Christian, the acknowledgment of God's existence, Jesus' resurrection, and the life we are called to live makes it a view that is absolutely relevant to my life.

The God-hypothesis we're testing is set within the biblical Judeo-Christian worldview and it passes the three tests of being logical, factual and livable.

9

The Essence of Life Resides Not in Chemistry But in (Organised) Information

In the first part of the book, we've reviewed five major 'gaps' in scientific knowledge. Of course, there are 'just so' stories of a universe creating itself out of nothing, the notion of so-called 'dark matter,' a warm pond with primordial chemicals, etc. But when we listen carefully to the true specialists at the top of their game, time and again we've heard the candid acknowledgement that mystery remains, a mystery we've labelled "magic" because the existence of a supernatural designer is ruled out from the start. And to escape such nonsense, we need only turn to the famous opening lines of the Bible: *"In the beginning God created the heavens and the earth"* (Genesis 1:1). This isn't magic because God, who is eternal and omnipotent, is a sufficient cause for the universe.

Despite having been compiled three and a half thousand years ago, this is still the most up-to-date account of origins that we have. As that does seem an extraordinary claim, we've been putting it to the test via a modern scientific approach of creating a hypothesis and then asking "If that's true, what predictions would it make?" We're then observing the evidence available to us to assess the accuracy or otherwise of the predictions made by the hypothesis: have they come to pass or have they failed? A fourth prediction would be: **That the essence of life resides not in chemistry but in (organized) information which can only be the product of intelligence and not chance.**

Cells – and our body perhaps has around 30 trillion of them – are like computers, and most of the workings of the cell are best described not in terms of material stuff – which we might call the hardware - but in terms of information or software. Which means that, as we've said, any attempt to make life just by mixing chemicals in a test tube is like soldering switches and wires in an attempt to produce Microsoft Windows. That's confusing hardware with software. Which leaves scientists (e.g. Paul Davies) to this very day still puzzling over how life could have arisen from non-living chemicals. The key question is how did the hardware of non-living molecules ever manage to write its own software?

Understanding the chemistry as we do still doesn't help us explain the origin of information. It's clear that the physical layout of letters on a printed page is independent of the chemical make-up of that printed page. A printed page of text is chemically identical to one of gobbledygook that uses all the same characters as before, only now they are shuffled. You know there's a difference. You can read one and it makes sense and gives a message, the other doesn't. But chemistry alone can't tell the difference.

It's also true that the physical order of the chemical DNA letters is independent of their chemistry. But it's precisely the arrangement of letters – either on a page or in our cells – that gives meaning and holds the vital information. And so it follows that chemistry experiments can never explain life's origin. Only the existence of God can explain the origin of information, and so atheism is indefensible.

The genetic code is the language of God, the language in which the information that constitutes life is written or encoded on molecules of DNA. Let's set this out clearly:

- As in human language, the cell employs a code specifically a four letter ("chemical bases") alphabet.
- As in human language, the cell organises its letters into words each word ("codon") being made up of 3 of those letters.
- As in human language, strings or phrases ("genes") made of words have an agreed meaning so that they can be recognised and translated. This agreed meaning is what we call the genetic code in which the words specify amino acids and the phrases of words specify proteins. We eat food rich in proteins, such as meat or eggs, and our digestive system breaks the proteins down into their building blocks, known as amino acids. These are then used by the cells in our bodies to construct new proteins. Although proteins are long chains of chemical molecules, known as polymers, it's not accurate - as we've demonstrated - to say life runs on chemicals. We're talking here about the intelligent or-

ganisation of these molecules with its information content. Genetic language is like human language, and there had to be intelligence capable of generating recognisable symbols and agreeing on their meaning. There are no such things as clever molecules.
- As in human language, punctuation is used so that theses phrases can be recognised.
- As in human language, words are organised into instructions that specify which one of the many possible proteins is to be made by copying a given gene.
- As in human language, the cell's language has a purpose: and that purpose is to construct protein sequences that will fold in specific ways or shapes to provide keys to unlock the operations of the cell.

Cells are like computers each running a code and the programming requires input from an intelligent designer. From the first chapter of the book of Genesis, the Bible talks about God speaking his creation into existence. It's hardly surprising then that we should find God's use of language reflected in his works in the natural world. Animals of all kinds communicate using symbols with agreed meanings. God, the creator and sustainer of all things, is a speaking God who uses language of one kind or another in all his interaction with the created order.

It is a wonderful fact that all physical life basically consists of language, language that is coded information. This information can be constructed, stored, communicated, interpreted and acted upon, and all this comes from the God who used language to speak things into existence. This explains how all life is based upon the same molecular mechanisms and the same genetic code. Where physical life is concerned, God speaks just one language that gives rise to a single genetic code expressed throughout a great diversity of creatures. The fact that we have this language in common is a pointer back to the unique super-intellect who spoke things into existence.

The findings of modern science clearly shows that the essence of life is not chemistry but intelligently organized information. That is, of course, a major prediction of the God-hypothesis, as we called it. The God-hypothesis is summed up most famously in the first ten words of the Bible: *"in the beginning God created the heavens and the earth."* And in the first chapter of Genesis we repeatedly come across the words: *"Then God said."* In this way, he spoke this marvelous universe of mathematical and molecular language into existence.

10

There Should be Irreducibly Complex Design Features

We have taken as our hypothesis: that the God of the Bible exists. Supposing this to be true, we ask ourselves: What would be its predictions? Another prediction, the fifth of those we are studying, is: **That there should be irreducibly complex design features.**

We have previously mentioned the example of the famous British philosopher and atheist, Sir Antony Flew. When he shocked the academic world by renouncing his atheism, one of the reasons he gave for denouncing atheism was the complexity of cellular life. Stuart Kauffman, an origins researcher, maintains that all organisms possess a property or feature known as minimum irreducibility. No less than Charles Darwin himself is on record as having stated that: "If it could be demonstrated that any complex organ existed which could not possibly have been formed by numerous, successive, slight modifications, my theory would absolutely break down." (Charles Darwin, *Origin of Species*).

THERE SHOULD BE IRREDUCIBLY COMPLEX DESIGN FEATURES

With this statement, Darwin provided a criterion by which his theory of evolution could be falsified. The logic was simple: since evolution is a gradual process in which slight modifications produce advantages for survival, it cannot produce complex structures suddenly or in a short amount of time. It's a step-by-step process which may gradually build up and modify complex structures, but it cannot produce them all at once. The man who coined the term "Big Bang," Sir Fred Hoyle, once made the categorical claim that life on earth had no simple small beginning. He talked of how even the allegedly most primitive lifeforms known to us, fossilised bacteria deep in the earth, were far from simple.

In more recent times, Michael Behe, a biochemical researcher and professor at Lehigh University in Pennsylvania, claims to have shown exactly what Darwin claimed would destroy the theory of evolution. He's done this through a concept he calls "irreducible complexity." In simple terms, this idea applies to any system of interacting parts in which the removal of any one part destroys the function of the entire system. An irreducibly complex system, then, requires each and every component to be in place before it will function.

As a simple example of irreducible complexity, Behe presents the humble mousetrap. It contains five interdependent parts which allow it to catch mice: the wooden platform, the spring, the hammer (that's the bar which crushes the mouse against the wooden base), the holding bar, and a catch. Each of these components is absolutely essential for the successful operation of the mousetrap. Without any one of its parts the whole system would not be fit for purpose. For instance, if you remove the catch, you cannot set the trap and it will never catch mice. Remove the spring, and the hammer will flop uselessly back and forth - certainly not much of a threat to the little rodents. Of course, removal of the holding bar will ensure that the trap never catches anything because there will again be no way to arm the system.

Now, let's think about what this implies: an irreducibly complex system cannot come about in a gradual manner. You can't begin with a wooden platform and catch a few mice, then add a spring, catching a few more mice than before, etc. No, all the components must be in place before it functions at all. A step-by-step approach to constructing such a system will result in a useless system until all the components have been added. The system requires all the components to be added at the same time, in the right setup, before it works at all.

How does irreducible complexity apply to biology? Behe notes that early this century, before biologists really understood the cell, they had a very simplistic model of its inner workings. Without the advanced techniques that now allow scientists to peer into the inner workings of the cell, it was assumed that the cell was a fairly simple blob, a "black box" – something that could be seen to perform various functions while its inner workings were unknown. Back then, it was easy to assume that the cell was a simple collection of molecules. But not any longer. Technological advances have provided detailed information about the inner workings of the cell.

Michael Denton, *in his book Evolution: A Theory in Crisis,* states "Although the tiniest bacterial cells are incredibly small ... each is in effect a veritable microminiaturized factory containing thousands of exquisitely designed pieces of intricate molecular machinery, made up altogether of one hundred thousand million atoms, far more complicated than any machine built by man and absolutely without parallel in the non-living world." In a word, the cell is complicated. Very complicated. In fact, Michael Behe goes on to claim that the complex biological structures in a cell demonstrate the same irreducible complexity we saw in the mousetrap example. In other words, they are all-or-nothing: either everything is there and it works, or something is missing and it doesn't work. As we saw before, such a system cannot be constructed in a gradual manner. It simply won't work until all the components are present, and Darwinism has no mechanism for adding all the components at once. Remember, Darwin's mechanism is one of gradual mutations leading to improved fitness and survival. A less-than-complete system of this nature simply will not function, and it certainly won't help the organism to survive. Indeed, having a half-formed and hence non-functional system would actually hinder survival and would be selected against.

But Behe is not the only scientist to recognize irreducible complexity in nature. In 1986, Michael J. Katz, (in his *Templets and the Explanation of Complex Patterns*, Cambridge: Cambridge University Press, 1986) wrote: "In the natural world, there are many pattern-assembly systems for which there is no simple explanation. There are useful scientific explanations for these complex systems, but the final patterns that they produce are so heterogeneous that they cannot effectively be reduced to smaller or less intricate predecessor components. As I will argue ... these patterns are, in a fundamental sense, irreducibly complex ..."

He continues saying that this sort of complexity is found in biology: "Cells and organisms are quite complex by all pattern criteria. They are built of heterogeneous elements arranged in heterogeneous configurations, and they do not self-assemble. One cannot stir together the parts of a cell or of an organism and spontaneously assemble a neuron or a walrus: to create a cell or an organism one needs a preexisting cell or a preexisting organism ..."

King David in one of his Bible psalms had this to say:

> *For You created my innermost parts;*
> *You wove me in my mother's womb.*
> *I will give thanks to You, because I am awesomely and wonderfully made;*
> *Wonderful are Your works,*
> *And my soul knows it very well.*
> *My frame was not hidden from You*
> *When I was made in secret,*
> *And skillfully formed in the depths of the earth;*
> *Your eyes have seen my formless substance;*
> *And in Your book were written*
> *All the days that were ordained for me,*
> *When as yet there was not one of them.*
> (Psalm 139:13-16)

That seems an apt description of how our body parts are intricately formed, indeed woven together, skillfully combined, each with its part to play. The Apostle Paul, writing in First Corinthians 12, seems to more than hint at the human body's irreducible complexity when he says: "*But now God has arranged the parts, each one of them in the body, just as He desired. If they were all one part, where would the body be? But now there are many parts, but one body. And the eye cannot say to the hand, 'I have no need of you'; or again, the head to the feet, 'I have no need of you.' On the contrary, it is much truer that the parts of the body which seem to be weaker are necessary ..."* (1 Corinthians 12:18-22). We are indeed awesomely and wonderfully made. Made in the image of God.

11

Time Had a Beginning

The expectation that **time had a beginning** is the last of our six selected predictions of the so-called "God-hypothesis" that we've been briefly exploring. The aim has been to show how all six of these basic and far-reaching predictions arising from this hypothesis have been resoundingly established by modern science.

The holy God of the Bible is said to inhabit eternity (Isaiah 57:15). That's one way in which God's "otherness" (that's the meaning of his "holiness") is demonstrated. For we are creatures of time, whereas he inhabits eternity. God himself exists outside of the created order of things. That means he's outside of time, just as Psalm 90 says – and this was a prayer of Moses to God – when he said *"Before the mountains were brought forth or ever you had formed the earth and the world even from everlasting to everlasting you are God."* And the Old Testament Bible prophet Isaiah (Isaiah 46:9) records God declaring: *"For I am God and there is no other; I am God and there is none like me declaring the end from the beginning."*

In the light of modern science, this may even begin to make more sense to us. Modern science now talks about space and time together as space-time. It implies that the whole of space-time must have a continuing existence. It seems natural to think of the whole of space having a continuing existence, but due to the space-time connection it's implied that the whole of time should have a continuing existence in the same way. That's quite intriguing. Think about it. We may go on a journey from A to B, and it's obvious to us when we arrive at place B, place A still exists. But if space and time are bound together in our modern understanding of the universe then this implies when we go from the past to arrive at the present, it means that the past still exists too. In any case, the Bible definitely declares that the past, the present and the future are all before God as the open landscape of time.

Another thing worth commenting on from modern science is that its equations and theories hold true no matter whether events run forwards or backwards in time. Nothing in the equations is sensitive to the direction of time. That is, apart from one law which is the law that governs growth in disorder. That only goes in one direction, and has led to this law being called "the arrow of time." Basically, it says something that I'm sure is consistent with all of our observations, and that is simply this: that things tend to wind down, becoming more and more disordered if left to themselves. If you find a classic car in a farmer's barn after it's been left there for 30 years, I think we all know it's going to take a lot of work to get it running like new again. And so this law of science that governs increasing disorder is one that tells us that to reverse it you have to put in a lot of work. You have to work hard to head back in the direction of making things more ordered again. You could say that science tells us what the future holds - and left to itself, that's going to be more and more disorder. For the arrow of time had to begin its flight in a highly ordered state of the early universe. (Scientists call that the low entropy condition of the early universe.)

That's about the only thing science can definitely tell us about the origin – that the universe was created in that way with a high level of order (or in a condition of low entropy). It cannot explain how it could have arrived in that condition other than something or someone somehow supplied energy or did work. Take the example of a humble elastic rubber band. When it lies crumbled up randomly on the table, it's highly disordered and has low energy content, pretty useless as far as being able to do any work. But now let me pick it up and stretch and twist it. It's now in an ordered shape and with stored energy. If it's connected to a propeller it can now make a model aeroplane fly as it unwinds, at the same time turning the propeller. But notice how someone, myself in this case, had to put in effort. I had to work to stretch and twist that rubber band into a higher state of order. And so we repeat: the arrow of time had to begin its flight in a highly ordered state of the early universe. And so, similarly, someone had to put in the work. Time – measured in this way in terms of the degree of order – had a beginning. This brings us back to God because he, and he alone, is unaffected by time's arrow. God is a God of order and he is the originator of order, even of all the order present in this universe.

Summing up, the state of science today validates what the Bible says when it talks of an eternity before the origin of the universe in which time could not exist. Time couldn't exist, because until the universe itself existed in some shape or form it could not be in any state of order or randomness. When the universe did come into existence, it must have been either created in a state of some order or put into such a state. Either way, that takes effort. It can't happen by itself, not spontaneously nor in any other way.

In other words, then, at a point in eternity an energetic act of creation must have occurred at some stage before time could begin to run for as time begins to run in the universe things begin to get less ordered. In effect, it begins to unwind, and that agrees with the Bible book of Hebrews when it says of created things, of the universe around us, that they will all grow old like a garment (Hebrews 1:11). And that's something it points out that's not true of the unchanging God.

Although some scientists have tried to model the universe as being without beginning (or end) in space and time, they have had to confess that in order to do this they must use tricks. Stephen Hawking, for example, introduced so-called "imaginary time." But as he himself says it's merely a mathematical device or trick so as to avoid a point of origin. He admits this doesn't work in real time. Does it not seem entirely reasonable then that we should allow ourselves to be guided by the flight of time's arrow, and not by such flights of fancy?

It was the historically famous theologian Augustine who said God created the universe with time, but not (embedded) in time. For him, it seems, not only the physical stuff of the universe had a finite beginning, but so did time itself. This, as we've seen, was an idea that was to become the modern orthodoxy:

that there was a beginning before which time did not exist. For the idea that time itself must have had a beginning is where science itself, as well as theology, gets to. When the amount of energy left that's available for useful work reaches its lowest possible value, we have also arrived at the point of total disorder. Plainly, we've not yet reached that point and so there cannot have been infinite time for decreasing order. For if time has been infinite the universe should by now already have become totally disordered and be in a state of complete chaos. This, thankfully, is not the case, so past time cannot be infinite. Therefore, time had a beginning.

And there are other ways to argue the same conclusion, namely that time has not been running for an infinite time. Take what's known as Olbers' Paradox. Olbers' Paradox says we should be bathed in light by now if the universe is eternal or very old. But the sky is not uniformly bright although it contains – to all intents and purposes – an infinite number of stars. In other words, if the universe were infinite in both age and size (with stars found throughout the universe), then the sky would not – should not - be dark at night. However, as we all know, it is.

And this is our sixth and final prediction of the God hypothesis - the prediction that there was a beginning before which time did not exist. It's easily shown to be true in that things get more disordered with time, and yet are not yet totally disordered, which must mean that time had a recent beginning. This shows us that the Bible's very first verse, Genesis 1:1, is still the most up-to-date account of origins that we have!

What we've seen overall has been five major "gaps" in scientific knowledge - the failures to explain (1) the origin of the universe, (2) the origin of stars, (3) the origin of life, (4) the origin of biodiversity, and (5) the origin of morality. If the existence of a supernatural designer is ruled out from the start, no other conclusive explanation remains. Our hypothesis was simply this: that the God of the Bible exists and that in the beginning he created the heavens and the earth. We proposed six major things that would be predicted if we took our stand on the first ten words of the Bible. These were that (1) we should not be able to find a material explanation for the origin of the universe; (2) that the universe should be rational and able to be understood by us; (3) that its laws should point to a lawgiver; (4) that life would be found to run on information not mere chemistry; (5) that lifeforms and organisms would be irreducibly complex (not capable of simple chance beginnings); and (6) finally that time itself should have a beginning. Put together, this argues for the biblical Judeo-Christian worldview being logical, factual and livable. And these are our usual ways to judge if something is true.

About the Author

Born and educated in Scotland, Brian worked as a government scientist until God called him into full-time Christian ministry on behalf of the Churches of God (www.churchesofgod.info). His voice has been heard on Search For Truth radio broadcasts for over 40 years (visit www.searchfortruth.podbean.com) during which time he has been an itinerant Bible teacher throughout the UK. His evangelical and missionary work outside the UK is primarily in Belgium, The Philippines and South East Central Africa. He is married to Rosemary, with a son and daughter.

More from Brian Johnston

If Atheism is True ... The Futile Faith and Hopeless Hypotheses of Dawkins and Co.

A former nuclear scientist turned missionary, Brian draws together previously published writings on apologetics to produce a concerted offensive against what the apostle Paul would surely describe as the 'indefensible' arguments of the so-called 'New Atheists'.

- CHAPTER 1 – INTRODUCTION
- CHAPTER 2: "ATHEISM MAKES MORE SENSE THAN CHRISTIANITY"
- CHAPTER 3: "WE DON'T NEED GOD TO CREATE LIFE ANYMORE!"
- CHAPTER 4: "THERE'S NO SUCH THING AS RIGHT OR WRONG"
- CHAPTER 5: "THE BIBLE IS JUST A BUNCH OF FAIRY STORIES"
- CHAPTER 6: "JESUS DIDN'T REALLY EXIST (AND EVEN IF HE DID, HE NEVER CLAIMED TO BE GOD!)"
- CHAPTER 7: "MADE IN GOD'S IMAGE? WE'RE JUST HIGHLY EVOLVED POND SCUM!"
- CHAPTER 8: "DEATH IS THE END AND THAT'S ALL THERE

IS TO IT"
- CHAPTER 9: "DESIGNED? THE UNIVERSE IS JUST A GIANT COSMIC ACCIDENT!"
- CHAPTER 10: "WE JUST HAVE TO ADMIT THAT THERE'S NO REAL PURPOSE TO LIFE"
- CHAPTER 11: "A REAL GOD WOULDN'T LET THE INNOCENT SUFFER"
- CHAPTER 12: "THE CHRISTIAN EXPERIENCE IS ONLY PSYCHOLOGICAL"
- CHAPTER 13: "THOSE SO-CALLED MIRACLES ARE SIMPLY IMPOSSIBLE"
- CHAPTER 14: "THE BIBLE IS FULL OF ERRORS AND CONTRADICTIONS"
- CHAPTER 15: "IT'S NONSENSE TO BELIEVE IN HELL AND A GOD OF LOVE!"
- CHAPTER 16: "SCIENCE HAS ELIMINATED THE NEED FOR FAITH"
- CHAPTER 17: "ALL THE BLOODSHED IN THE NAME OF RELIGION IS JUST HYPOCRISY"
- CHAPTER 18: "THERE'S NO SUCH THING AS OBJECTIVE TRUTH"
- CHAPTER 19: AN APPEAL FROM COOKIES

Does Anyone Know Why We're Here? Answers from Ecclesiastes

A Christian apologist, was once speaking to a large college crowd when he was suddenly interrupted. A student stood up and yelled, "Everything is meaningless!" He responded, "You don't believe that." The student yelled back, "Yes, I do!" "No, you don't." "I most certainly do. Who are you to tell me I don't?" "Then repeat your statement for me." "Everything is meaningless!" He then said, "If your statement is meaningful, then everything is not meaningless. On the other hand, if everything is meaningless, then what you have just said is meaningless too. So, in effect, you have said nothing. You can sit down."

The consideration of whether it could be true that everything is meaningless is not a consideration we expect to find arising from within a biblical worldview, where God is accepted as existing and giving meaning and purpose to human existence. But the curious thing – at least at first sight – is that one entire book in the Bible is devoted to exploring whether or not everything is meaningless. Why should this be the case? Bible teacher and broadcaster Brian Johnston gives the answer.

About Hayes Press

Hayes Press (www.hayespress.org) is a registered charity in the United Kingdom, whose primary mission is to disseminate the Word of God, mainly through literature. It is one of the largest distributors of gospel tracts and leaflets in the United Kingdom, with over 100 titles and many thousands dispatched annually. In addition to paperbacks and eBooks, Hayes Press also publishes Plus Eagles' Wings, a fun and educational Bible magazine for children, and Golden Bells, a popular daily Bible reading calendar in a desk or wall format.

If you would like to contact Hayes Press, there are a number of ways you can do so:

By mail: c/o The Barn, Flaxlands, Royal Wootton Bassett, Wiltshire, UK SN4 8DY

By phone: 01793 850598

By eMail: info@hayespress.org

via Facebook: www.facebook.com/hayespress.org

www.ingramcontent.com/pod-product-compliance
Lightning Source LLC
Chambersburg PA
CBHW061340040426
42444CB00011B/3010